Little People, BIG DREAMS
BRUCE LEE

Written by
Mª Isabel Sánchez Vegara

Illustrated by
Miguel Bustos

Frances Lincoln
Children's Books

This is the story of a little boy born in San Francisco. His parents named him Lee Jun-Fan, but the nurse at the hospital gave him the name that became famous: Bruce.

He was a young boy when his family moved back to Hong Kong, where his dad was a well-known opera star. Soon, Bruce followed in his footsteps and became a child actor.

Bruce was a lazy student who didn't like going to school much. But he was very interested in martial arts. He wanted to learn the secrets of wing chun, a sort of kung fu, taught by an old grandmaster.

Bruce was good at almost anything: from boxing
and fencing to dancing the cha-cha, a Latin dance that
everybody wanted to learn—and that he grew up to master.

But Bruce also had a talent for fighting on the streets and messing with the local gangs. One day, his parents decided to send him back to America to keep him out of trouble.

The night before his departure, Bruce made a promise to become a better person. He knew that mistakes can be forgiven, if one has the courage to admit them.

He crossed the Pacific Ocean as a cha-cha teacher, and
once in the US, he studied philosophy and got
a job teaching wing chun to his fellow students.

Once he graduated, Bruce opened three martial arts schools on the West Coast, where he mixed the best of what he had learned to create his own combat method: Jeet Kune Do.

He was so fast that one time he knocked out an opponent with 15 punches and a kick in a fight that only lasted 11 seconds! It was said he could catch a grain of rice in midair with his chopsticks.

Bruce got a part in a TV series, but he struggled to make it to the big screen in Hollywood. So, he returned to Hong Kong, where he was offered the main role in his first martial arts movie.

He fought with the grace of a dancer and the charm of an actor. And soon, he was even writing, directing, and producing his own movies.

Bruce made martial arts so popular that Hollywood finally gave him the opportunity he had longed for. He became the most famous Asian American movie star ever, when he played "Lee" in *Enter the Dragon*, the king of kung fu movies.

And by having faith in himself and never giving up,
little Bruce became a hero for everyone, and the
person he always dreamed he would be.

BRUCE LEE

(Born 1940 • Died 1973)

c. 1940s

1959 (top right)

Lee Jun-Fan came into the world in the year of the Dragon, in a hospital in San Francisco. He was given the English name "Bruce" by a nurse. His parents were on tour there with the Chinese opera, but in the 1940s, they moved back to Hong Kong. His dad was an opera star, and Bruce followed in his starry footsteps to act in films—around 20 in his childhood alone. Bruce was also a natural dancer. His fancy footwork and skillful balance won him a cha-cha dance title in Hong Kong. But as a teenager, Bruce hung around with local street gangs and learned kung fu as a form of protection. His parents were worried, so they sent him to America to live with family friends. In America, Bruce took up work as a dance instructor and finished high school. He then enrolled in college to study philosophy, while also teaching martial arts. Bruce eventually opened his own martial

c.1970

1973

arts school. He loved teaching his students in a style he called Jeet Kune Do. It was a mixture of ancient kung fu, fencing, boxing, and philosophy. After giving a demonstration at a tournament, Bruce attracted the attention of television bosses. He was cast in a TV series called *The Green Hornet* as a sidekick. After the series was canceled, Bruce struggled to find acting work. So, he moved to Hong Kong and starred in films that broke box office records. He used this success to form his own production company and wrote, directed, and starred in his own films. One, *Enter the Dragon*, became a US box office smash and made Bruce an international movie star. Sadly, he died suddenly after it was made. Bruce is now credited as the actor, director, martial artist, and philosopher who changed Asian representation in 20th-century American film.

Want to find out more about **Bruce Lee?**
Read one of these great books:

Who Was Bruce Lee? by Jim Gigliotti and John Hinderliter

Boys Who Made a Difference by Michelle Roehm McCann

You could even ask for lessons in Bruce Lee's Jeet Kune Do style of martial arts.

BOARD BOOKS

AMELIA EARHART

ISBN: 978-1-84780-888-2

AGATHA CHRISTIE

ISBN: 978-1-84780-960-5

MARIE CURIE

ISBN: 978-1-84780-962-9

ROSA PARKS

ISBN: 978-1-78603-018-4

AUDREY HEPBURN

ISBN: 978-1-78603-053-5

EMMELINE PANKHURST

ISBN: 978-1-78603-020-7

ELLA FITZGERALD
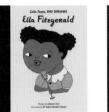
ISBN: 978-1-78603-087-0

ADA LOVELACE

ISBN: 978-1-78603-076-4

JANE AUSTEN

ISBN: 978-1-78603-120-4

GEORGIA O'KEEFFE

ISBN: 978-1-78603-122-8

HARRIET TUBMAN

ISBN: 978-1-78603-227-0

ANNE FRANK

ISBN: 978-1-78603-229-4

MOTHER TERESA

ISBN: 978-1-78603-230-0

JOSEPHINE BAKER

ISBN: 978-1-78603-228-7

L. M. MONTGOMERY
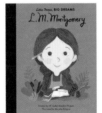
ISBN: 978-1-78603-233-1

JANE GOODALL

ISBN: 978-1-78603-231-7

SIMONE DE BEAUVOIR

ISBN: 978-1-78603-232-4

MUHAMMAD ALI
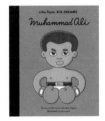
ISBN: 978-1-78603-331-4

STEPHEN HAWKING

ISBN: 978-1-78603-333-8

MARIA MONTESSORI

ISBN: 978-1-78603-755-8

VIVIENNE WESTWOOD

ISBN: 978-1-78603-757-2

MAHATMA GANDHI

ISBN: 978-1-78603-787-9

DAVID BOWIE

ISBN: 978-1-78603-332-1

WILMA RUDOLPH

ISBN: 978-1-78603-751-0

DOLLY PARTON

ISBN: 978-1-78603-760-2

BRUCE LEE

ISBN: 978-1-78603-789-3

RUDOLF NUREYEV

ISBN: 978-1-78603-791-6

Brimming with creative inspiration, how-to projects, and useful information to enrich your everyday life, Quarto Knows is a favorite destination for those pursuing their interests and passions. Visit our site and dig deeper with our books into your area of interest: Quarto Creates, Quarto Cooks, Quarto Homes, Quarto Lives, Quarto Drives, Quarto Explores, Quarto Gifts, or Quarto Kids.

First Published in the UK in 2019 by Frances Lincoln Children's Books, an imprint of The Quarto Group.

400 First Avenue North, Suite 400, Minneapolis, MN 55401, USA.

T (612) 344-8100 F (612) 344-8692 **www.QuartoKnows.com**

First Published in Spain in 2019 under the title Pequeño & Grande Bruce Lee by Alba Editorial, s.l.u., Baixada de Sant Miquel, 1, 08002 Barcelona

www.albaeditorial.es

Published by arrangement with Alba Editorial, s.l.u. Translation rights arranged by IMC Agència Literària, SL

A catalog record for this book is available from the British Library.

ISBN 978-1-78603-789-3

The illustrations were created in pencil and colored digitally.

Set in Futura BT.

Published by Rachel Williams • Designed by Karissa Santos

Edited by Katy Flint • Production by Jenny Cundill

Manufactured in Guangdong, China CC052019

9 7 5 3 1 2 4 6 8

Photographic acknowledgments (pages 28–29, from left to right) 1. Bruce Lee as a child, c. 1940s © Everett Collection Inc / Alamy Stock Photo 2. Bruce Lee and family, c. 1959 © Michael Ochs Archives / Handout via Getty Images 3. Photo of Bruce Lee, c. 1970 © Michael Ochs Archives / Stringer via Getty Images 4. Enter the Dragon, 1973 © Michael Ochs Archives / Stringer via Getty Images

HONG KONG

BRUCE ♥ LEE

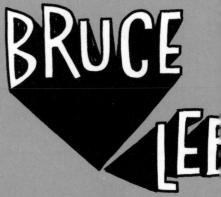

THE GREEN HORNET